FRIGATES
of the
ROYAL CANADIAN NAVY
1943 - 1974

Ken Macpherson

Vanwell Publishing Limited

St. Catharines, Ontario

Macpherson, Ken
  Frigates of the Royal Canadian Navy 1943 - 1974

Bibliography: p.
Includes index.
ISBN 0-920277-22-5

1. Frigates — Canada — History — 20th century.
I. Title.

V826.5.C3M3 1988   359.3'254'0971   C88-095134-6

Distributed in Britain by
Tri-Service Press; Ltd.
Shrewsbury, SY1 1JE England

CONTENTS

FOREWORD

To those who were not actually there, mention of the great days of the Royal Canadian Navy in World War II conjures visions of small, single-gunned corvettes endlessly bouncing and searching about silent columns of merchant ships ploughing the North Atlantic, in convoy. Corvettes typified Canada's naval contribution to the Battle of the Atlantic wherein, without question, they played a magnificent role. But it is extraordinary that one seldom hears of the finest anti-submarine vessels built in Canada during the entire war: frigates. Perhaps it is because the first of the 107 Canadian-built corvettes, HMCS *Collingwood*, was commissioned in late 1940 and she and the other corvettes bore the brunt of those first terrible years, while the first of 60 Canadian-built frigates, HMCS *Waskesiu*, was not commissioned until June, 1943.

Excellent books have been written of corvettes, such as James B. Lamb's *The Corvette Navy*, and Thomas K. Lynch's *Canada's Flowers*; and of the armed yachts pressed into service in the urgent circumstances of the early years of the war, such as Fraser M. McKee's *The Armed Yachts of Canada*. Even the motor launches had their day in print, albeit not complementarily, in MacLean's *Fairmiles and Foul*. But of frigates, seldom a word until Ken Macpherson took up his pen.

To put them into perspective, it should be realized that not only were frigates sleek of line, but they were equipped with the finest anti-submarine devices then available in this country and so became the most effective naval vessels built in Canada, especially for anti-submarine warfare. Such equipment included the ARL plotting table, with its dot of light which moved with the ship's course and speed, shining through a glass top and large sheet of plain paper to enable the ship's movements to be traced, and Asdic and radar contacts to be plotted as they occurred,

during attacks, thus presenting a total picture of what was happening and providing a record for later analysis.

Frigates were the first Canadian-built warships to be fitted with the 147B "Sword" protruding below the hull to determine the depth of underwater targets by a horizontal fan of transmissions and returning echoes, while the regular Asdic obtained the range and bearing with a similar, but vertical fan. Thereby, both horizontal and vertical pinpointing of submerged targets was possible. The data thus obtained were sent to operators of the latest anti-submarine weapon, the Hedgehog, a device which fired 24 projectiles in an elliptical pattern ahead of the attacking vessel, while still in Asdic contact. Unlike depth-charge attacks, in which the charges were dropped over the stern and fired from either beam at a target since lost by the Asdic operator, the Hedgehog projectiles would explode only when one made contact, with lethal effect on a U-boat. Only too often, depth-charges set to explode at a predetermined depth, created such an upheaval in the water, whether hitting or missing, that the target could escape behind the wall of water turbulence.

Frigates were also first with four power-mounted, twin Oerlikon guns, close-range weapons lethal against crews emerging from U-boat conning towers. These ships also mounted twin (Massey Harris-built) 4-inch guns, allowing double the illumination of surfaced night targets and twice the forward firepower of any lesser escort vessel.

The quantity of ammunition carried in frigates far surpassed that of any other Canadian A/S ship, including, as well as 4-inch and 3-inch after gun shells and Hedgehog projectiles, 150 depth-charges for the prolonged attacks made possible by the great cruising range of these ships.

In addition to first-class radar, the frigate had the critical HF/DF ("Huff-Duff") device

to obtain bearings on U-boat W/T transmissions. At some distance apart, the hunters could fix the target's position by obtaining cross-bearings of his transmissions.

Yes, frigates were outstanding anti-submarine vessels and important contributors to victory over the U-boats. Ken Macpherson's foresight in writing their story before it fades from memory has saved for posterity yet another piece of this country's history.

The honour done me by Ken asking me to write a Foreword is matched only by the enthusiasm with which I do so. Read on, now, and see why. Read about frigates . . . .

C. Ian P. Tate
"Topsail"
Kinmount, Ont.

Ian Tate was one of only two officers to survive the sinking of HMCS Valleyfield, the only Canadian frigate lost during the war.

INTRODUCTION

When Canada entered the war on September 10, 1939, her entire naval escort force consisted of six destroyers, and efforts had to be made to augment this force quickly through domestic construction. The escort type initially chosen was the Flower class corvette, and considerable numbers of these were produced in a surprisingly short time. They had been designed only for coastal use, but nothing better was available in sufficient numbers for Atlantic convoys, and so they were thrust into the role of ocean escorts until a more suitable type could be developed.

This type was the frigate, initially dubbed "twin-screw corvette" and designed by William Reed, O.B.E., of Smith's Dock Company, South Bank-on-Tees. The first orders were placed by the Royal Navy under the 1940 Programme, and Smith's Dock's *Rother* was the first completed, in April 1942. Like her 56 sisters, she was named for a river in Britain. The name "frigate" was adopted later that year at the suggestion of Vice-Admiral Percy Nelles, Canada's Chief of Naval Staff.

Reed's design won immediate favour with Ottawa, and construction of 30 frigates in Canadian yards had been approved by October 1941. The only real drawback lay in their being too long to transit the St. Lawrence canal system, so that they could not be built on the Great Lakes as many corvettes and minesweepers had been. All were built in west coast and St. Lawrence River yards. Canadian members of the class were nearly all named for cities or towns, but bore the "River class" designation despite some slight confusion with the RCN's River class destroyers.

First in service: HMCS Waskesiu, 1943.

Waskesiu before she was commissioned — a photo frequently misidentified. The clouds were added in the darkroom.

In the end, 33 frigates were built for the RCN under the 1942-43 Programme, and 27 more under the 1943-44 Programme. Of a further 10 built for the Royal Navy, two found their way into the USN and became prototypes of its 77-ship City class. It has also been stated that these two, with modifications, provided the basic design for the USN's huge WW2 destroyer escort programme.

Seven River class sisters were taken over from the RN in 1944, along with three of the Loch class — a somewhat larger version designed for prefabrication.

The frigate, 301 feet long, must have seemed palatial to those who had served their apprenticeship in corvettes. Its twin engines gave it only three knots' advantage in speed, but its range — 7200 miles at 12 knots — was nearly double that of its smaller consort. It also carried a much more effective outfit of anti-submarine equipment, including the only twin 4-inch gun in any Canadian ship smaller than a Tribal class destroyer.

The River class ships were late entrants in the Battle of the Atlantic, the first commissioned being *Waskesiu* in June 1943, but they immediately proved their worth as ocean escorts. Singly or in company, they took part in the destruction of 12 U-boats. Only one of the class, *Valleyfield*, became a war loss, though three others were so badly damaged in action as not to have been considered worth repairing.

Most of these ships were taken in hand after VE Day for "tropicalization", with a view to service in the Pacific, but few had completed the process by VJ Day. Shortly after the war, in what somehow seems a fit of profligacy, eleven of them were stripped and sunk as breakwaters for B.C. logging firms, and eight others summarily scrapped.

In postwar years, however, the class was extensively used as training ships, and between 1953 and 1958 the remaining 21 of them underwent extensive renovation from which they emerged flush-decked members of what was termed the Prestonian class. The large, low quarterdeck was now roofed in to house two Squid anti-submarine mortars; the wheelhouse was much enlarged and the funnel heightened accordingly. As redesigned they were less attractive ships, but doubtless more practical. The last of these units, *Victoriaville*, took over the name and duties of the retiring diving tender *Granby* in 1966, and was sold for scrap in 1974.

As noted earlier, the Canadian frigates entered the war after the tide of the Atlantic battle had turned for good against the Kriegsmarine. For this reason few of them received the kind of media accolade that was lavished upon the corvettes.

Nonetheless, it was to these ships that a majority, one suspects, of seagoing personnel recruited in the latter half of the war were drafted. Certainly most of the new entries and cadets of the two decades after the war learned their trades in frigates. It is to these and, more especially, the youngsters of the 1940s, now middle-aged like me, that this book is dedicated.

KRM
Port Hope, 1988

Penetang's *quarterdeck in the spring of 1945, the corvette* ***Thorlock,*** *a fellow-member of EG C-9, crossing her wake. Note the storage rack with depth charge reloads for the throwers.*

*HMCS **Strathadam**'s engine room. The Chief ERA keeps an eye on the telegraph while the stoker behind him tends the throttle.*

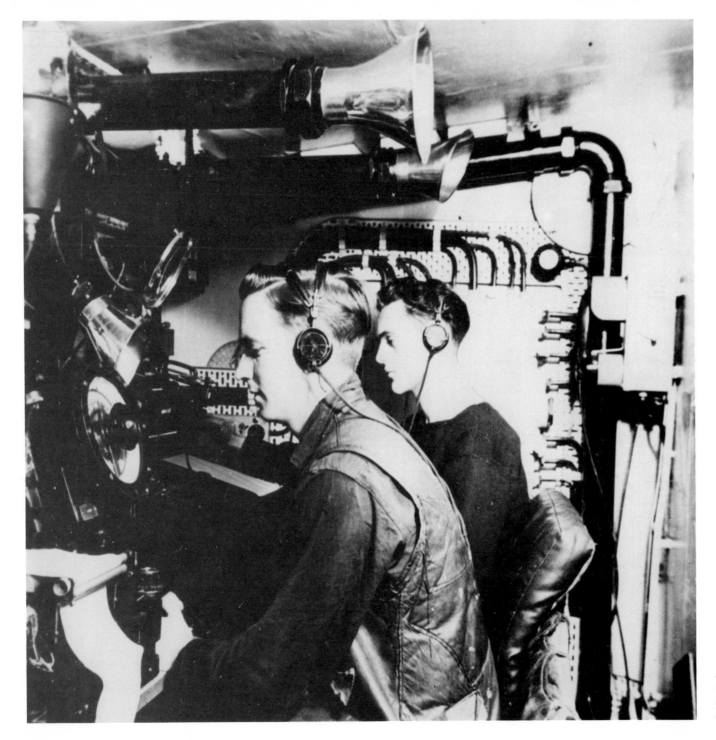

Strathadam's Asdic "hut". Operators are identified as Norm Henderson and Frank Lindsay.

Strathadam's stokers' mess, with the usual card game in progress beneath slung hammocks.

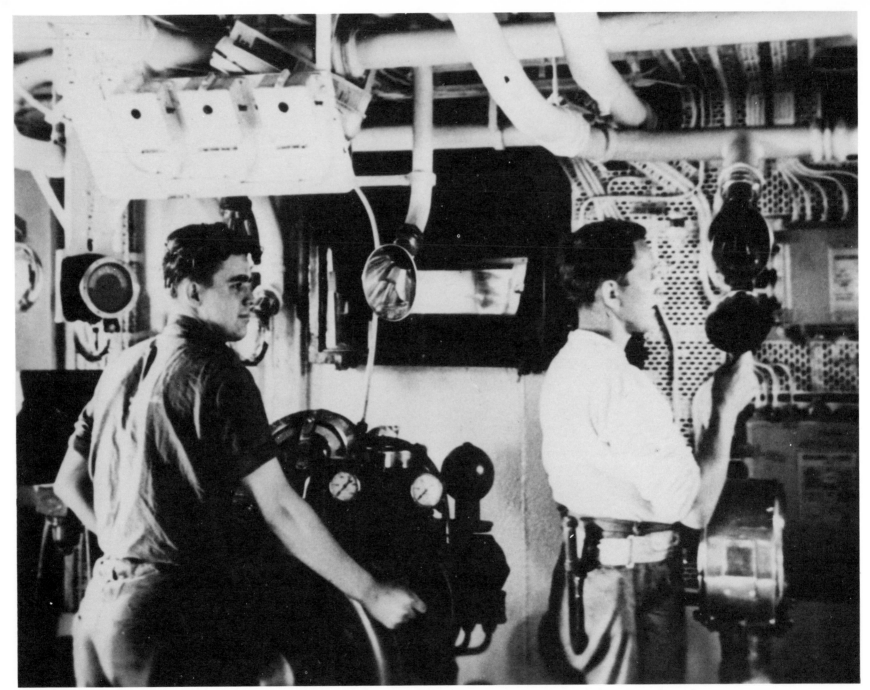

Strathadam's wheelhouse, with crewmen identified as Hawley and Zinc. The quartermaster could see ahead only by means of a periscope.

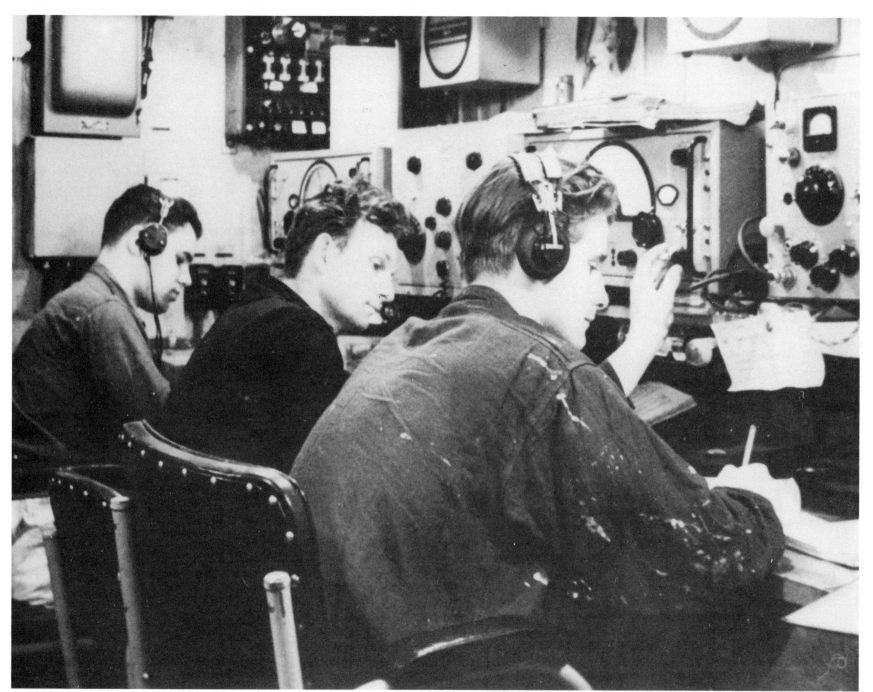

Strathadam's wireless "shack".

A close-up of an unidentified frigate gives good detail of wheelhouse and bridge structure.

	wartime pendant	postwar pendant		wartime pendant	postwar pendant
BEACON HILL	K407	303	*NEW GLASGOW	K320	315
CAP de la MADELEINE	K663	317	NEW WATERFORD	K321	304
*CAPE BRETON	K350		ORKNEY	K448	
CHARLOTTETOWN	K244		*OUTREMONT	K322	310
CHEBOGUE	K317		*PORT COLBORNE	K326	
*DUNVER	K05		*PRINCE RUPERT	K324	
EASTVIEW	K665		*ST. CATHARINES	K325	324
*GROU	K518		*SAINT JOHN	K456	
JOLIETTE	K418		SPRINGHILL	K323	
JONQUIERE	K318	318	STETTLER	K681	311
KIRKLAND LAKE	K337		*STORMONT	K327	
KOKANEE	K419		*SWANSEA	K328	306
La HULLOISE	K668	305	THETFORD MINES	K459	
LONGUEUIL	K672		*VALLEYFIELD	K329	
MAGOG	K673		*WASKESIU	K330	
*MATANE	K444		WENTWORTH	K331	
*MONTREAL	K319				

Displacement: 2,216 tons (full load)

Dimensions: 301'6'' x 36'7'' x 12'9'' (mean)

Complement: 8 officers, 133 other ranks

Armament (original): 1 twin 4-inch gun; 1 12-pdr.; 4 twin 20-mm guns in paired mounts; Hedgehog; 4 D.C. throwers, 2 traps, 150 - 200 depth charges.

*Note: the 15 ships marked above were completed with a single 4-inch gun fore and aft but, with the exception of the lost *Valleyfield*, later received the twin 4-inch mount.

Armament as Prestonians: 1 twin 4-inch gun; 6 40-mm guns (one twin, 4 singles); 2 Squid mortars.

BEACON HILL

Builder: Yarrows Ltd., Esquimalt, B.C.

Launched November 6, 1943.

Commissioned May 16, 1944 at Esquimalt.

Wartime career: attached to EG 26 in September. On support and patrol duties out of Londonderry, Plymouth and Portsmouth. Returned to Canada end of May 1945 and was paid off at Esquimalt February 6, 1946.

Postwar career: recommissioned June 16, 1949 for cadet training. Converted to Prestonian class escort, 1954-57, recommissioning as such December 21, 1957. Paid off for the last time on September 15, 1967.

Fate: broken up at Sakai, Japan, in 1968.

Remarks: was named for Victoria, B.C., whose name itself could not be used because of potential confusion with HMS *Victorious*.

*A fine study of a brand-new frigate: **Beacon Hill** in B.C. waters, June 5, 1944.*

◄ *Beacon Hill as reconstructed 1954-57. The photo is dated March 9, 1959.*

CAP de la MADELEINE

Builder: Morton Engineering & Dry Dock Co., Quebec City.

Launched May 13, 1944.

Commissioned September 30, 1944 at Quebec City.

Wartime career: assigned to EG C-7 in December 1944 but made only one partial Atlantic crossing, having to turn back for repairs. VE Day intervened before these were completed and she was paid off November 25, 1945.

Postwar career: sold to Marine Industries Ltd. but reacquired for conversion to Prestonian class escort. Recommissioned as such on December 7, 1954 for cadet and new entry training on the east coast. Paid off for the last time on May 15, 1965.

Fate: broken up in 1966 at La Spezia, Italy.

Cap de la Madeleine after reconstruction, on June 8, 1959. The flush deck is particularly apparent in contrast to the photo below.

Cap de la Madeleine off Quebec City in the summer of 1944.

CAPE BRETON

Builder: Morton Engineering & Dry Dock Co., Quebec City.

Launched November 24, 1942.

Commissioned October 25, 1943 at Quebec City.

Wartime career: assigned to EG 6 in February 1944. On support and patrol duties out of Londonderry, Plymouth and Portsmouth. Made one round trip to Murmansk, and was present on D Day. Transferred to EG 9 in May 1945 after a six-month refit in Canada, but sailed direct from 'Derry to Vancouver after VE Day. She was paid off January 26, 1946 after some months in reserve at Esquimalt.

Fate: was sold in 1947 and expended as part of a breakwater, reportedly at Kelsey Bay, B.C.

Remarks: was named for Sydney, N.S., whose name itself was reserved for the Royal Australian Navy.

Cape Breton at Londonderry in 1944.

Cape Breton off Quebec City in 1943, before she was commissioned. Lacking a clinker screen to her funnel, and with only a single 4-inch gun forward, she exemplifies the appearance of the first 15 frigates completed.

*By now sporting a twin 4-inch gun, **Cape Breton** is seen here during the winter of 1944-45, in the course of her long refit at Shelburne, N.S.*

CHARLOTTETOWN

Builder: Davie Shipbuilding & Repairing Co. Ltd., Lauzon, Quebec.

Launched September 16, 1943.

Commissioned April 28, 1944 at Quebec City.

Wartime career: assigned in June 1944 to EG 16, and was transferred with the group to Londonderry in March 1945. In May, made two round trips with Gibraltor convoys, then sailed for Canada for tropicalization refit. Sailed for Esquimalt in March 1946 and spent the remainder of the year on training duties. Was paid off March 25, 1947.

Fate: sold in 1947 and expended as part of a breakwater at Oyster Bay, B.C.

Remarks: this ship was given both the name and the pendant number (K244) of the corvette *Charlottetown*, lost in September 1942.

Charlottetown in June 1944.

*Recently arrived on the west coast, **Charlottetown** with reservists embarked for training, May 7, 1946.*

CHEBOGUE

Builder: Yarrows Ltd., Esquimalt, B.C.

Launched August 17, 1943.

Commissioned February 22, 1944 at Esquimalt.

Wartime career: assigned in May 1944 to EG C-1 and made three crossings with Atlantic convoys that summer. On her third crossing, with westbound convoy ONS.33, she was torpedoed by *U 1227* on October 4, losing most of her quarterdeck. Towed to Port Talbot, Wales, she was paid off September 25, 1945. Eventually adjudged not worth repairing, she was scrapped locally in 1948.

Remarks: was named for Yarmouth, N.S., whose name itself had already been assigned to a British naval base.

Chebogue in March 1944, shortly before sailing for the east coast. The camouflage is typical of the west coast-built frigates.

Chebogue after being torpedoed October 4, 1944.

DUNVER

Builder: Morton Engineering & Dry Dock Co., Quebec City.

Launched November 10, 1942.

Commissioned September 11, 1943 at Quebec City.

Wartime career: assigned in November to EG C-5, and served continuously as a mid-ocean escort until October 1944. Among 16 Atlantic convoys escorted was HXS.300 in July 1944, the largest convoy of the war with 167 ships. On September 9, while on patrol with HMCS *Hespeler*, she assisted in sinking *U 484* near convoy ONF.252. In April 1945, was transferred to EG 27, Halifax. In June, went to the west coast and was finally paid off January 23, 1946.

Fate: expended in 1948 as part of a breakwater at Royston, B.C.

Remarks: was named, in a strange fashion, for Verdun, Quebec, the name itself already being that of an RN destroyer. *Dunver* was the first frigate launched for the RCN.

Dunver in 1944, wearing the funnel markings of Escort Group C-5.

Dunver, again probably in 1944. This fine view shows to full advantage the very large depth-charge armament carried in these ships.

EASTVIEW

Builder: Canadian Vickers Ltd., Montreal.

Launched November 17, 1943.

Commissioned June 3, 1944 at Montreal.

Wartime career: assigned in August 1944 to EG C-5 as Senior Officer's ship, and spent the remainder of the European war as a mid-ocean escort. Her 13th and last convoy, HX.358, was also the last HX convoy of the war, sailing late in May 1945. That July *Eastview* went to the west coast, where she was paid off January 17, 1946.

Fate: sold in 1947, and her hull made part of a breakwater at Oyster Bay, B.C., the following year.

Remarks: was named for Ottawa, whose name itself could not be used because of the existing HMCS *Ottawa*, named for the river.

◄ *Eastview in 1944, very new.*

▼ *Eastview hove-to at sea, occasion unknown.*

Eastview's ship's company assembled for the customary group portrait. She is berthed at St. John's, likely in the spring of 1945.

GROU

Builder: Canadian Vickers Ltd., Montreal.

Launched August 7, 1943.

Commissioned December 4, 1943 at Montreal.

Wartime career: assigned in March 1944 to EG 6, and in April made a round trip to Murmansk. Operated at different times from Londonderry, Portsmouth and Plymouth, and was present on A/S patrol on D Day. *Grou* returned to Canada in February 1945, and that October left for the west coast. Was paid off into reserve at Esquimalt February 25, 1946.

Fate: broken up at Victoria in 1946.

Remarks: was named for Pointe-aux-Trembles, Quebec, but the name itself was considered too long. Grou was a French martyr of 1690 associated with the locality.

Grou was one of those unfortunates who seem to take an indifferent picture. This one probably shows her on arrival in Halifax in February 1945.

▼ *Grou, probably at Montreal in December 1943.*

JOLIETTE

Builder: Morton Engineering & Dry Dock Co., Quebec City.

Launched November 12, 1943.

Commissioned June 14, 1944 at Quebec City.

Wartime career: assigned in August 1944 to EG C-1, but on reaching Londonderry the following month was reassigned to EG 25. On November 22 she grounded in Lough Foyle, receiving severe bottom damage, and was under repair at Belfast until early April 1945. *Joliette* returned to Canada in June, and was paid off at Sydney on November 19.

Fate: sold in 1946 to the Chilean Navy and renamed *Iquique*. Disposed of in 1968.

*The unusual flag hoist suggests that **Joliette** is celebrating VE Day.*

***Joliette** off Quebec City in the summer of 1944, perhaps on July 1, the day she left for Halifax.*

JONQUIERE

Builder: Davie Shipbuilding & Repairing Co. Ltd., Lauzon, Quebec.

Launched October 28, 1943.

Commissioned May 10, 1944 at Quebec City.

Wartime career: assigned in August to EG C-2, and after three Atlantic crossings was reassigned to EG 26. Served out of Londonderry, Plymouth and Portsmouth on support and patrol duties. Sailed on May 27, 1945 with ON.305, the last westbound convoy of the war, and was paid off December 4 at Shelburne, N.S.

Postwar career: converted by her original builder to a Prestonian class escort and recommissioned as such on September 20, 1954, for training purposes on the west coast. Paid off for the last time September 12, 1966.

Fate: broken up at Victoria, B.C. in 1967.

Jonquière in December 1958, as rebuilt to Prestonian class configuration.

Jonquière at Quebec City in May 1944.

KIRKLAND LAKE

Builder: Morton Engineering & Dry Dock Co., Quebec City.

Launched April 27, 1944.

Commissioned August 21, 1944 at Quebec City.

Wartime career: assigned in December to EG 16 and accompanied the group in March 1945 to Londonderry when it was transferred there. Operated at various times out of Portsmouth as well, and in May 1945 escorted two convoys to Gibraltar and two back. Returned to Canada in June and was paid off into reserve at Halifax on December 14, 1945.

Fate: broken up at Sydney, N.S., 1947-48.

Kirkland Lake in the St. Lawrence, shortly before she was commissioned in August 1944.

28

KOKANEE

Builder: Yarrows Ltd., Esquimalt, B.C.

Launched November 27, 1943.

Commissioned June 6, 1944 at Esquimalt.

Wartime career: assigned in September to EG C-1 as Senior Officer's ship, and spent the remainder of the European war on Atlantic convoy duty. Her 14th and last crossing was made with westbound convoy ON.304 late in May 1945. Was paid off into reserve on the west coast December 21.

Fate: sold in 1948 to the government of India for conversion to a Hooghly River pilot vessel and renamed *Bengal*.

Remarks: was named for Nelson, B.C., whose name itself could not be used because of the battleship HMS *Nelson*.

◄ *Kokanee, another brand-new west coast product, on June 23, 1944.*

For contrast, the same ship in 1945, with Escort Group C-3's badge on her funnel.

La HULLOISE

Builder: Canadian Vickers Ltd., Montreal.

Launched October 29, 1943.

Commissioned on May 20, 1944 at Montreal.

Wartime career: assigned in July 1944 to EG 16, Halifax, but reassigned in October to EG 25 and transferred with it to Londonderry in November. Based variously at 'Derry and Rosyth for the rest of the European war. On March 7, 1945, with *Strathadam* and *Thetford Mines*, shared in the sinking of *U 1302* in St. George's Channel. Returned to Canada late in May and was paid off at Halifax on December 6.

Postwar career: recommissioned June 24, 1949 for cadet and new entry training on the east coast. Again recommissioned Oct. 9, 1957 after conversion to Prestonian class configuration. Paid off for the last time on July 16, 1965.

Fate: broken up at La Spezia, Italy in 1966.

Remarks: the ship was named for Hull, Que., whose name itself could not be used owing to confusion with USS *Hull*.

*A magnificent study of one of these "warriors for the working day": **La Hulloise** berthing at Liverpool, England, in 1945.* ▶

*Little altered since the war, **La Hulloise** on July 20, 1950 — a photo of some sentimental significance to the author, who was aboard at the time.*

La Hulloise as reconstructed 1953-57. The photo was taken October 16, 1958.

LONGUEUIL

Builder: Canadian Vickers Ltd., Montreal.

Launched October 30, 1943.

Commissioned on May 18, 1944 at Montreal.

Wartime career: was assigned in July 1944 to EG C-2, and spent the remainder of the European war on convoy duty in the north Atlantic. At various times Senior Officer's ship, she made 14 crossings. *Longueuil* returned to Canada in June 1945 and was paid off December 31 at Esquimalt.

Fate: sold in 1947 and reportedly expended at Kelsey Bay, B.C., as part of a breakwater.

*Both photos show **Longueuil** in 1945.*

MAGOG

Builder: Canadian Vickers Ltd., Montreal.

Launched September 22, 1943.

Commissioned on May 7, 1944 at Montreal.

Wartime career: assigned in August 1944 to EG 16, and engaged in escort and patrol duty in the vicinity of Halifax, Sydney and Gaspé. While escorting convoy GONS.33 on October 14, 1944, she was torpedoed off Pointe des Monts in the St. Lawrence River by *U 1223*. Lacking 60 feet of her stern, *Magog* was adjudged a constructive total loss and paid off December 20.

Fate: Broken up in 1947.

◄ *Magog with her stern blown off by an acoustic torpedo, October 14, 1944.*

*Magog in fall of 1944, photographed from her sister-ship, **Stettler**, on patrol in the St. Lawrence.*

MATANE

Builder: Canadian Vickers Ltd., Montreal.

Launched May 29, 1943.

Commissioned October 22, 1943 at Montreal.

Wartime career: joined EG 9 at Londonderry in April 1944 as Senior Officer's ship and thereafter served mainly on patrol duties in U.K. waters. A recent reassessment credits her, with *Swansea*, for the sinking of *U 311* on April 22. Was present at D Day. On July 20, was hit off Brest by a glider bomb and towed to Plymouth by *Meon*. On May 13, 1945, following lengthy repairs, *Matane* sailed to escort convoy JW.67 to north Russia, but was detached on May 16 to help escort 14 surrendered U-boats from Trondheim to Loch Eriboll. In June, after a round trip to Gibraltar, she proceeded direct from Londonderry to Esquimalt. There, on February 11, 1946, she was paid off into reserve.

Fate: expended as part of a breakwater at Oyster Bay, B.C. in 1948.

Down by the stern after being hit by a glider bomb on July 20, 1944, **Matane** *is assisted by* **Meon**.

Matane in June 1944.

MONTREAL

Builder: Canadian Vickers Ltd., Montreal.

Launched June 12, 1943.

Commissioned November 12, 1943 at Montreal.

Wartime career: assigned in February 1944 to EG C-4, and was employed until the fall of that year as mid-ocean escort to 12 Atlantic convoys. In September she was transferred to EG 26 at Londonderry and thereafter remained in U.K. waters. On December 17, 1944 she rescued survivors of *U 1209*, which had been wrecked near Land's End. She returned to Canada at the end of March 1945 for tropicalization refit, then carried out miscellaneous duties out of Halifax until paid off into reserve on October 15.

Fate: sold in 1947 and broken up at Sydney, N.S.

*A ship whose paint job seems to have been unique, was **Montreal**. She has a simulated clipper bow and bow wave.*

*Since the above photo was taken, **Montreal** has acquired a conventional funnel cap, but still has only single 4-inch armament.*

NEW GLASGOW

Builder: Yarrows Ltd., Esquimalt, B.C.

Launched May 5, 1943.

Commissioned December 23, 1943 at Esquimalt.

Wartime career: allocated in April 1944 to EG C-1 and served as escort to seven Atlantic convoys before being reassigned in September to EG 26. Thereafter served in U.K. waters out of Londonderry, Portsmouth and Plymouth until the end of the European war. On March 21, 1945, she rammed and sank *U 1003* off Lough Foyle, and was herself laid up for repairs until early June. She then returned to Canada and was paid off into reserve on November 5.

Postwar: recommissioned January 30, 1954 after conversion to Prestonian class escort, and carried out training duties until finally paid off at Esquimalt on January 30, 1967.

Fate: broken up in Japan in 1967.

New Glasgow in 1945.

▼ *New Glasgow in January 1944.*

Providing a first-rate portrayal of the changes made while under reconstruction, **New Glasgow** *as a Prestonian class unit in 1954.*

NEW WATERFORD

Builder: Yarrows Ltd., Esquimalt, B.C.

Launched July 3, 1943.

Commissioned January 21, 1944 at Victoria.

Wartime career: assigned in May 1944 to EG 6 as a replacement for the damaged *Teme*, and for the remainder of the European war carried out patrol duties out of Londonderry, Portsmouth and Plymouth. Returned to Canada for tropicalization refit at Liverpool, N.S., then sailed for the west coast, where she was paid off into reserve on March 7, 1946.

Postwar career: commissioned during much of 1953 as accommodation vessel at Esquimalt, then underwent conversion to a Prestonian class escort. Recommissioned as such on January 31, 1958 and served in a training capacity until finally paid off December 22, 1966.

Fate: broken up in 1967 at Savona, Italy.

New Waterford before proceeding to the east coast in February 1944.

New Waterford after conversion, on February 24, 1958.

ORKNEY

Builder: Yarrows Ltd., Esquimalt, B.C.

Launched September 18, 1943.

Commissioned April 18, 1944 at Victoria.

Wartime career: assigned in August 1944 to EG 16 but transferred in October as Senior Officer's ship to EG 25 at Londonderry, and thereafter remained in U.K. waters. On February 13, 1945, collided with and sank S.S. *Blairnevis*. Repairs to *Orkney* took until mid-April, and the ship sailed for Canada late in May. She was paid off into reserve on January 22, 1946.

Postwar career: sold in 1947, she became for a time the Israeli immigrant ship *Violetta* before joining the Israeli Navy as *Mivtakh*. Sold in turn in 1950 to the Sri Lankan Navy, she was renamed *Mahasena*. Broken up at Singapore in 1964.

◄ *Orkney while working up in Bermuda, July 1944.*

***Orkney** before leaving the west coast in May 1944.*

OUTREMONT

Builder: Morton Engineering & Dry Dock Co., Quebec City.

Launched July 3, 1943.

Commissioned November 27, 1943 at Quebec City.

Wartime career: assigned in February 1944 to EG 6, Londonderry, and served for the remainder of the European war principally on escort and patrol duties in U.K. waters. She was present at D Day, and made one trip to north Russia. She returned to Canada in December 1944 and, soon after completing tropicalization refit, was paid off November 5, 1945 and sold to Marine Industries Ltd. Later reacquired and converted to a Prestonian class escort, she served as a training ship from September 2, 1955 until June 7, 1965, when she was paid off for disposal.

Fate: broken up at La Spezia, Italy, in 1966.

Outremont at Sydney in mid-1945. She has been fitted with SU type radar at her foremasthead, necessitating the erection of a mainmast for the HF/DF antenna.

Outremont in Prestonian guise on October 16, 1958. She carries a gunnery target on her quarterdeck.

PORT COLBORNE

Builder: Yarrows Ltd., Esquimalt, B.C.

Launched April 21, 1943.

Commissioned November 15, 1943 at Victoria.

Wartime career: assigned in April 1944 to EG 9 at Londonderry, escorting convoy HXM.289 en route there. She remained in U.K. waters, except for one round trip to north Russia in December, and was present at D Day. Left for Canada in February 1945, completing tropicalization that fall, and was paid off into reserve at Halifax November 7.

Fate: broken up at Sydney, N.S. in 1947.

◄ *Port Colborne in 1944.*

Port Colborne on the same occasion.

PRINCE RUPERT

Builder: Yarrows Ltd., Esquimalt, B.C.

Launched February 3, 1943.

Commissioned August 30, 1943 at Esquimalt.

Wartime career: joined EG C-3 as Senior Officer's ship in January 1944, and spent the balance of the European war on convoy duty in the north Atlantic. On March 13, 1944, she assisted in sinking *U 575*. She escorted 16 convoys before being transferred to EG 27 in the spring of 1945. That June she went to the west coast, and there was paid off January 15, 1946.

Fate: sold in 1947, and her hull expended as part of a breakwater at Royston, B.C. In September 1985, 74 former crew members held a reunion at the site.

Prince Rupert in 1944; two views on the same occasion.

ST. CATHARINES

Builder: Yarrows Ltd., Esquimalt, B.C.

Launched December 5, 1942.

Commissioned July 31, 1943 at Esquimalt.

Wartime career: assigned in October to EG C-2. Spent the following year in the north Atlantic, escorting 16 convoys. On the passage of one of these, HX.280, she assisted in the destruction of *U 744* on March 6, 1944. She was Senior Officer's ship of the group from February to September 1944. She returned to Canada that September to undergo a very long refit, including tropicalization, by the end of which the European war was over, and was paid off November 18, 1945.

Postwar career: converted to a weather ship and stationed in the north Pacific, 1952-67.

Fate: broken up in Japan in 1968.

◄ *St. Catharines in 1944.*

St. Catharines with a convoy in 1943 or '44.

SAINT JOHN

Builder: Canadian Vickers Ltd., Montreal.

Launched August 25, 1943.

Commissioned December 13, 1943 at Montreal.

Wartime career: joined EG 9 at Londonderry in April 1944. She was on hand at D Day. On September 1, 1944 she and *Swansea* sank *U 247*, and on February 16, 1945 *Saint John* destroyed *U 309* in Moray Firth. She made one round trip to north Russia in December 1944, returning to Canada the following spring. Paid off into reserve at Halifax, November 27, 1945.

Fate: broken up at Sydney, N.S. in 1947.

Saint John photographed from an RCAF patrol plane on March 13, 1944.

Saint John in May 1944. The totally different paint jobs, neither new, in the two-month interval, are difficult to understand.

44

SPRINGHILL

Builder: Yarrows Ltd., Esquimalt, B.C.

Launched September 7, 1943.

Commissioned March 21, 1944 at Victoria.

Wartime career: joined EG 16, Halifax, as Senior Officer's ship in August, and transferred with the group to Londonderry in March 1945. Returned to Canada in April for tropicalization at Pictou, N.S. Paid off into reserve at Halifax, December 1, 1945.

Fate: broken up in 1947 at Sydney, N.S.

Springhill on March 7, 1945. She had left Halifax that day for Londonderry.

Springhill in July 1944, while working up in Bermuda.

STETLER

Builder: Canadian Vickers Ltd., Montreal.

Launched September 10, 1943.

Commissioned May 7, 1944 at Montreal.

Wartime career: assigned to EG 16, Halifax, in July, and carried out local escort duties until March 1945, when the group was transferred to Londonderry. Thereafter employed in U.K. waters except for two round trips to Gibraltar in May and June of 1945. Left 'Derry for home June 16, the last Canadian warship to do so. Paid off November 9, 1945.

Postwar career: sold but reacquired and converted to Prestonian class escort, recommissioning as such February 27, 1954. Served in a training role until finally being paid off on the west coast, August 31, 1966.

Fate: broken up at Victoria, B.C. in 1967.

Remarks: was intended to honour Edmonton, but the name itself could not be used because of potential confusion with HMCS *Edmundston*.

Stettler as modernized, in January 1966, her last year in service.

Stettler when new, in May 1944.

46

STORMONT

Builder: Canadian Vickers Ltd., Montreal.

Launched July 14, 1943.

Commissioned November 27, 1943 at Montreal.

Wartime career: joined EG 9 at Londonderry in March 1944, and was on hand at D Day. Made a round trip to Gibraltar in October 1944 and to Murmansk in December. Returned to Halifax at the end of the year and was paid off there on November 9, 1945.

Fate: sold in 1947 to a Montevideo buyer, but resold in 1951 and converted at Kiel as Aristotle Onassis' luxury yacht *Christina*.

Remarks: was named for Cornwall, Ont., whose actual name could not be used because of confusion with HMS *Cornwall*.

Top left: **Stormont** *being disarmed for disposal, in September 1945.*

*This 1944 photo of **Stormont** is, sad to say, the best at-sea view that could be found of her.*

*Who would recognize **Stormont** under the sleek skin of Onassis' yacht **Christina**?*

SWANSEA

Builder: Yarrows Ltd., Esquimalt, B.C.

Launched December 19, 1942.

Commissioned October 4, 1943 at Victoria.

Wartime career: assigned to EG 9, Londonderry, and made her passage there with convoy SC.154, taking part in the sinking of *U 845* en route, on March 10, 1944. On April 14 she sank *U 448* in company with HMS *Pelican*, and on April 22, assisted by HMCS *Matane*, disposed of *U 311*. Was present on D Day, and thereafter on post-invasion A/S patrol. On September 1, with *Saint John*, sank *U 247*. Returned to Canada for tropicalization refit, following which she was paid off November 2, 1945.

Postwar career: engaged during most of 1948-53 in cadet and new entry training. Rebuilt, 1953-57, as a Prestonian class escort, and resumed her training role on the west coast until paid off for the last time October 14, 1966.

Fate: broken up at Savona, Italy in 1967.

Swansea in January 1944.

▼ *Swansea on September 12, 1949.*

48

*Under circumstances like these, the word "enemy" frequently seemed to lose much of its meaning. Survivors of **U 448** cling to the gunwale of **Swansea's** whaler, April 14, 1944.*

Swansea was the only frigate among Canada's representatives at Queen Elizabeth's Coronation Naval Review, June 15, 1953.

Swansea, converted to a Prestonian class unit, about 1959.

THETFORD MINES

Builder: Morton Engineering & Dry Dock Co., Quebec City.

Launched October 30, 1943.

Commissioned May 24, 1944 at Quebec City.

Wartime career: assigned to EG 25 and transferred with the group to Londonderry in November, 1944, escorting convoy HX.317 en route. On A/S patrol duty out of 'Derry and Rosyth until VE-Day. On March 7, 1945 she assisted in sinking *U 1302* in St. George's Channel, *La Hulloise* and *Strathadam* being the other participants. On May 11 she escorted eight surrendered U-boats into Lough Foyle. Returned to Canada late in May and was paid off November 18 at Sydney.

Fate: sold in 1947 to a Honduran buyer.

Thetford Mines in the St. Lawrence in May 1944.

▲ *Thetford Mines* at Londonderry on May 11, 1945. She had just escorted eight surrendered U-boats there.

VALLEYFIELD

Builder: Morton Engineering & Dry Dock Co., Quebec City.

Launched July 17, 1943.

Commissioned December 7, 1943 at Quebec City.

Wartime career: allocated to EG C-1. Detached from her first convoy, SC.154, to escort the disabled rescue ship *Dundee* to Horta, in the Azores. From there, in March 1944, escorted the damaged HMCS *Mulgrave* in tow for the Clyde. On May 7, 1944, *Valleyfield* was torpedoed SE of Cape Race by *U 548*, soon after leaving convoy ONM.234, and sank very quickly with the loss of 125 lives. She was the only RCN member of her class to be lost.

Valleyfield in drydock at Halifax on January 17, 1944, being checked for ice damage after passage from Montreal.

Valleyfield in the St. Lawrence in December 1943, with visitors from Valleyfield aboard.

WASKESIU

Builder: Yarrows Ltd., Esquimalt, B.C.

Launched December 6, 1942.

Commissioned June 16, 1943 at Victoria.

Wartime career: the first RCN frigate to enter service, she joined EG 5 in Londonderry in November. The group was renumbered EG 6 the same month. *Waskesiu* served chiefly in U.K. waters, but supported Gibraltar and Sierra Leone convoys early in 1944, and in April made a round trip to Murmansk. On February 24, while escorting convoy SC.153, she had sunk *U 257*. She was present on D Day. Returned to Canada for a lengthy refit in September, and was again briefly stationed at 'Derry before proceeding to the west coast in June 1945. She was paid off into reserve on January 29, 1946.

Fate: sold to the government of India in 1947; converted to pilot vessel *Hooghly*.

Remarks: was named for Prince Albert, Sask., whose name could not be used verbatim because of confusion with HMS *Prince Albert*.

Waskesiu on June 16, 1943, the day she was commissioned.

Likely the first photo of a Canadian frigate to be released: Waskesiu on builder's trials in the early summer of 1943.

Waskesiu in a U.K. port, 1944.

WENTWORTH

Builder: Yarrows Ltd., Esquimalt, B.C.

Launched March 6, 1943.

Commissioned December 7, 1943 at Victoria.

Wartime career: joined EG C-4 in June 1944, becoming Senior Officer's ship in August, and remained continuously on convoy duty until February 1945. She made seven round trips across the Atlantic. Was paid off into reserve on October 10, 1945.

Fate: broken up in 1947 at Sydney, N.S.

◄ *Wentworth in May 1944, working up in St. Margaret's Bay.*

Wentworth in Juan de Fuca Strait, January 3, 1944.

*An excellent close-up of **Wentworth** in mid-1944, her Hedgehog showing to particular advantage.*

1943 - 44 PROGRAMME

	wartime pendant	postwar pendant		wartime pendant	postwar pendant
ANTIGONISH	K661	301	POUNDMAKER	K675	
BUCKINGHAM	K685	314	PRESTONIAN	K662	307
CAPILANO	K409		ROYALMOUNT	K677	
CARLPLACE	K664		RUNNYMEDE	K678	
COATICOOK	K410		ST. PIERRE	K680	
FORT ERIE	K670	312	ST. STEPHEN	K454	323
GLACE BAY	K414		STE. THERESE	K366	
HALLOWELL	K666		SEA CLIFF	K394	
INCH ARRAN	K667	308	STONE TOWN	K531	302
LANARK	K669	321	STRATHADAM	K682	
LASALLE	K519		SUSSEXVALE	K683	313
LAUZON	K671	322	TORONTO	K538	319
LEVIS	K400		VICTORIAVILLE	K684	320
PENETANG	K676	316			

Displacement: 2,216 tons (full load)

Dimensions: 301'6'' x 36'7'' x 12'9'' (mean)

Complement: 8 officers, 133 other ranks

Armament (original): 1 twin 4-inch gun; 1 12-pdr.; 4 twin 20-mm guns in paired mounts; Hedgehog; 4 D.C. throwers, 2 traps, 150 - 200 depth charges.

Armament as Prestonians: 1 twin 4-inch gun; 6 40-mm guns (one twin, 4 singles); 2 Squid mortars.

ANTIGONISH

BUILDER: Yarrows Ltd., Esquimalt, B.C.

Launched February 10, 1944.

Commissioned July 4, 1944 at Victoria.

Wartime career: assigned in October to EG 16, and transferred with it to Londonderry in March 1945. On patrol and support duty for the next three months, including two trips to Gibraltar. Returned to Canada in June for tropicalization refit at Pictou, and in December went to Esquimalt, where she was paid off into reserve on February 5, 1946. Converted, 1956 - 57, to Prestonian class escort and served as a training ship for cadets and new entries until finally paid off on November 30, 1966.

Fate: broken up in Japan in 1968.

Antigonish preparing to ''cheer ship'' on the occasion of a Royal Visit to the west coast, October 27, 1951.

▼ *Antigonish during workups in Bermuda, October, 1944.*

Antigonish on November 11, 1957, after modernization.

BUCKINGHAM

Builder: Davie Shipbuilding & Repair Co. Ltd., Lauzon, Quebec.

Launched April 28, 1944.

Commissioned November 2, 1944 at Quebec City.

Wartime career: assigned in February 1945 to EG 28, carrying out patrol and escort duty out of Halifax until VE Day. Escorted the surrendered *U 889* to Shelburne, N.S. in mid-May. Paid off into reserve on November 16.

Postwar career: sold to Marine Industries Ltd. in 1946, but reacquired and converted to a Prestonian class escort, 1953 - 54. Recommissioned June 25, 1954 and served a training role until paid off for the last time on March 23, 1965.

Fate: broken up at La Spezia, Italy, in 1966.

Remarks: *Buckingham,* fitted with a helicopter deck, carried out trials, October - December 1956, preliminary to the development of the RCN's first destroyer helicopter carriers.

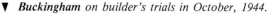

▼ *Buckingham on builder's trials in October, 1944.*

Buckingham during helicopter trials in 1956. The landing deck was fitted only temporarily.

CAPILANO

Builder: Yarrows Ltd., Esquimalt, B.C.

Launched April 8, 1944.

Commissioned August 25, 1944 at Victoria.

Wartime career: assigned in November to EG C-2 at St. John's, and spent the rest of the European war as a mid-ocean escort, making nine trips across the Atlantic before returning to Canada in June 1945. Paid off into reserve on November 24, 1945, following tropicalization refit.

Fate: sold in 1947, and in 1948 appears under Jamaican registry as S.S. *Irving Francis M.* Foundered in 1953 off Cuba while en route from Jamaica to Miami in tow of *Bess Barry M.*, the former HMCS *St. Boniface.*

Remarks: was named for North Vancouver, whose actual name could not be used for fear of confusion with HMCS *Vancouver.*

Capilano on September 9, 1944, soon after leaving for the east coast.

▼ *Capilano picking up castaways in April 1945.*

61

CARLPLACE

Builder: Davie Shipbuilding & Repairing Co. Ltd., Lauzon, Quebec.

Launched July 6, 1944.

Commissioned December 13, 1944 at Quebec City.

Wartime career: suffered ice damage to her hull on route to Halifax, necessitating several weeks' work there and at Philadelphia. Following workups in Bermuda, was assigned in April to EG 16, Londonderry. She had only time for a round trip to Gibraltar before the European war ended, and she returned to Canada for tropicalization refit. This was called off when VJ Day intervened, and she was paid off at Halifax on November 13, 1945.

Fate: sold to the Dominican Republic in 1946 for conversion to a presidential yacht, she was renamed *Presidente Trujillo* and, in 1962, *Mella*.

Remarks: her name was an abbreviation of Carleton Place, Ont.

Carlplace (left) and Sussexvale, presumably while undergoing tropicalization refit at Shelburne, N.S., in the summer/fall of 1945.

Carlplace in 1945.

COATICOOK

Builder: Davie Shipbuilding & Repairing Co. Ltd., Lauzon, Quebec.

Launched November 26, 1943.

Commissioned July 25, 1944 at Quebec City.

Wartime career: assigned in September to EG 27, Halifax, she served on escort and patrol duties from that base for the duration of the European war. Went to Esquimalt in June 1945 and was paid off into reserve there on November 29.

Fate: sunk in 1949 as part of a breakwater at Powell River, B.C., but refloated in 1961 and taken to Victoria to be broken up. It was feared, however, that she would sink in harbour before she could be scrapped, and so she was scuttled off Race Rocks on December 14, 1961.

◄ *Coaticook in December 1944.*

A port-quarter view of Coaticook on the same occasion.

*Still in her builder's hands, **Coaticook** in the St. Lawrence in the summer of 1944. Utility combined with gracefulness!*

FORT ERIE

Builder: George T. Davie & Sons Ltd., Lauzon, Quebec.

Launched May 27, 1944.

Commissioned October 27, 1944 at Quebec City.

Wartime career: assigned in January 1945 to EG 28, Halifax, for the remainder of the European war. Tropicalization refit at Pictou was suspended that August, and the ship was paid off November 22.

Postwar career: reacquired from Marine Industries Ltd., to whom she had been sold in 1946, and rebuilt, 1954 - 55, as a Prestonian class escort. Served as a training ship during most of the period between April 17, 1956 and March 26, 1965, when she was paid off at Halifax.

Fate: broken up at La Spezia, Italy, in 1966.

Fort Erie in 1945.

Fort Erie as modernized 1954 - 55. The photo is dated October 16, 1959.

GLACE BAY

Builder: George T. Davie & Sons Ltd., Lauzon, Quebec.

Launched April 26, 1944.

Commissioned September 2, 1944 at Lévis, Quebec.

Wartime career: assigned in October to EG C-4, Londonderry, and worked her passage there in November as escort to a number of U.S.-built subchasers destined for the Russian Navy. Employed from then until VE Day in the north Atlantic, where she escorted ten convoys. Returned to Canada in June 1945 for miscellaneous duties out of Halifax. Paid off November 17 at Sydney.

Fate: sold in 1946 to the Chilean Navy and renamed *Esmeralda,* then, in 1952, *Bacquedano.* Broken up in 1968.

Glace Bay while working up in Bermuda, October 1944.

▼ *Glace Bay* off Quebec City, September 1944.

HALLOWELL

Builder: Canadian Vickers Ltd., Montreal.

Launched March 28, 1944.

Commissioned August 8, 1944 at Montreal.

Wartime career: assigned in November to EG C-1, and was Senior Officer's ship from December onward. Continuously employed until the end of the European war as a mid-ocean escort, making nine crossings before leaving for Canada in June 1945. In July and August, ferried returning military personnel from St. John's to Canada. Paid off into reserve November 7, 1945.

Fate: sold to Uruguayan interests in 1946, but resold in 1949 to become the Israeli immigrant ship *Sharon*. Acquired in 1952 by the Israeli Navy and renamed *Misnak*. Sold to the Sri Lankan Navy in 1959 and renamed *Gajabahu*. Discarded in 1978.

Remarks: was named for Picton, Ont., whose actual name could not be used because of probable confusion with HMCS *Pictou*.

◄ *Hallowell (right),* **Arnprior** *and, probably,* **HMS Ness,** *at Londonderry in May 1945.*

Hallowell, probably in the fall of 1944.

67

INCH ARRAN

Builder: George T. Davie & Sons Ltd., Lauzon, Quebec.

Launched June 6, 1944.

Commissioned November 18, 1944 at Quebec City.

Wartime career: assigned in January 1945 to EG 28, and spent the remainder of the European war on escort and patrol duties out of Halifax. Escorted the surrendered *U 889* into Shelburne, N.S. on May 13, 1945. Paid off into reserve on November 28.

Postwar career: reacquired in 1951 from Marine Industries Ltd., who had purchased her in 1946. Recommissioned August 23, 1954, after conversion to a Prestonian class escort, and performed a training role on the east coast until finally paid off June 23, 1965.

Fate: acquired by the Kingston, Ont., Master Mariners' Association for conversion into a museum and youth club, but the project failed to materialize and she was broken up in 1970.

Remarks: named for Dalhousie, N.S., whose name could not be used because of HMIS *Dalhousie*.

Inch Arran on acceptance trials near Quebec City, November 18, 1944, the day she was commissioned.

Inch Arran on December 10, 1959, after rebuilding to a Prestonian class escort.

LANARK

Builder: Canadian Vickers Ltd., Montreal.

Launched December 10, 1943.

Commissioned July 6, 1944 at Montreal.

Wartime career: assigned in October to EG C-7, Londonderry, and spent the remainder of the European war as a mid-ocean escort, for the most part as Senior Officer's ship. She escorted 12 Atlantic convoys before returning to Canada in June 1945. Paid off into reserve October 24.

Postwar career: reacquired from Marine Industries Ltd., who had bought her in 1946, and recommissioned April 26, 1956 after rebuilding as a Prestonian class escort. Served as a training ship on the east coast until finally paid off March 16, 1965.

Fate: broken up at La Spezia, Italy in 1966.

Remarks: named for Perth, Ont., whose name itself could not be used because of HMAS *Perth*.

◄ *Lanark at Londonderry in 1945.*

Lanark, 1944 - 45.

Lanark on May 30, 1960 as converted to a Prestonian class escort.

LASALLE

Builder: George T. Davie & Sons Ltd., Lauzon, Quebec.

Launched November 12, 1943.

Commissioned June 29, 1944 at Quebec City.

Wartime career: assigned in October to EG 27, Halifax, and spent the remainder of the European war on patrol and support duty locally. Went to the west coast in June 1945, and was paid off there on December 17.

Fate: expended as part of a breakwater at Kelsey Bay, B.C., in 1948.

Lasalle in September 1944, while working up in Bermuda.

Lasalle on February 20, 1945 with a convoy, probably FH.158. ▶

LAUZON

Builder: George T. Davie & Sons Ltd., Lauzon, Quebec.

Launched June 10, 1944.

Commissioned August 30, 1944 at Quebec City.

Wartime career: allocated to EG C-6 in November and was thereafter employed as a mid-ocean escort until VE Day. Escorted nine Atlantic convoys. Returned to Canada in June 1945 and served that summer as a troop-carrier between St. John's and Quebec City. Paid off into reserve November 7.

Postwar career: sold in 1946 to Marine Industries Ltd. but reacquired in 1951 for conversion into a Prestonian class escort. Recommissioned as such December 12, 1953 and served as a training ship on the east coast until finally paid off May 24, 1963.

Fate: sold for scrap in 1964.

Lauzon coming alongside a sister at Halifax, December 16, 1953. ►

A very poor photo of Lauzon, the best of the only three that could be located of her at sea in wartime.

LEVIS

Builder: George T. Davie & Sons Ltd., Lauzon, Quebec.

Launched November 26, 1943.

Commissioned July 21, 1944 at Quebec City

Wartime career: assigned in September to EG 27, and spent the balance of the European war on patrol and escort work out of Halifax. Sailed for the west coast at the end of 1945, having completed tropicalization refit at Lunenburg. Paid off into reserve at Esquimalt, January 30, 1946.

Fate: expended as part of a breakwater at Oyster Bay, B.C. in 1948.

Remarks: was the second of her name to serve in the RCN, the first having been a corvette lost in 1941.

Lévis at the port for which she was named, apparently on the day of her commissioning, July 21, 1944.

Lévis at sea, 1944 - 45.

PENETANG

Builder: Davie Shipbuilding & Repairing Co. Ltd., Lauzon, Quebec.

Launched July 6, 1944.

Commissioned October 19, 1944 at Quebec City.

Wartime career: allocated in February 1945 to EG C-9, Londonderry, and by VE Day had escorted seven Atlantic convoys. Returned to Canada in June 1945 to serve for a time as a troop-carrier between St. John's and Quebec City. Paid off November 10, 1945.

Postwar career: sold to Marine Industries Ltd. in 1945, but reacquired for conversion to a Prestonian class escort, recommissioning June 1, 1954 for training purposes. Lent in 1956 to the Norwegian Navy and renamed *Draug,* she was transferred outright three years later and broken up in 1966.

Remarks: despite some indignation on the part of the town for which she was named, the full name, Penetanguishene, was considered too long.

Penetang off Halifax, November 8, 1954.

Penetang off Quebec City in the fall of 1944.

*A fine study of **Penetang** in March 1945.*

POUNDMAKER

Builder: Canadian Vickers Ltd., Montreal.

Launched April 21, 1944.

Commissioned September 17, 1944 at Montreal.

Wartime career: assigned in December to EG C-8, St. John's, and served as a mid-ocean escort until VE Day. She made eight round trips across the Atlantic with convoys. Soon after completion of tropicalization refit at Lunenburg, on November 25, 1945, she was paid off at Sydney.

Fate: sold in 1947 to the Peruvian Navy, to be renamed *Teniente Ferre* and, in 1963, *Ferre*. She was broken up in 1966.

Remarks: was named for North Battleford, whose actual name could not be used because of corvette HMCS *Battleford*.

Poundmaker in 1944, brand-new, and unusual as a ▶ *Montreal-built ship in that she wears west coast-type camouflage.*

Poundmaker in 1945, wearing the funnel markings of EG C-8.

Poundmaker in 1945.

PRESTONIAN

Builder: Davie Shipbuilding & Repairing Co. Ltd., Lauzon, Quebec.

Launched June 22, 1944.

Commissioned September 13, 1944 at Quebec City.

Wartime career: assigned in January 1945 to EG 28, Halifax, and was employed locally until VE Day. Paid off at Halifax on November 9.

Postwar career: reacquired from Marine Industries Ltd., to whom she had been sold, and converted to become the name-ship of the Prestonian class. Was recommissioned as such August 22, 1953. Paid off April 24, 1956, for loan to the Norwegian Navy, and renamed *Troll.* Transferred outright in 1959 and, in 1965, reclassified as submarine depot ship and renamed *Horten.* Discarded in 1972 and scrapped.

Remarks: named for Preston, Ont., whose actual name could not be used because of HMS *Preston.*

Prestonian here exemplifies the modernized appearance of the class to which she gave her name.

Prestonian on September 9, 1944, while still fitting out at Lauzon. She was commissioned four days later. Wartime photos of this ship are scarce.

ROYALMOUNT

Builder: Canadian Vickers Ltd., Montreal.

Launched April 15, 1944.

Commissioned August 25, 1944 at Montreal.

Wartime career: allocated in November to EG C-1, and spent the rest of the European war on convoy duty, making ten trips across the Atlantic. After a long refit at Sydney, was paid off November 17, 1945.

Fate: sold for scrap in 1947.

Remarks: was named for Mount Royal, but the actual name might have been confused with that of frigate *Montreal*.

Royalmount in rough weather, 1944 - 45.

Royalmount viewed from an RCAF aircraft, 1945.

Runnymede just launched at Montreal, November 27, 1943.

RUNNYMEDE

Builder: Canadian Vickers Ltd., Montreal.

Launched November 27, 1943.

Commissioned June 14, 1944 at Montreal.

Wartime career: assigned in August to EG C-5 as Senior Officer's ship and was employed for the remainder of the European war as a mid-ocean escort. She escorted 14 convoys before returning to Canada in June 1945. Went to the west coast that summer and was paid off January 19, 1946.

Fate: sold in 1947 and reportedly expended as part of a breakwater at Kelsey Bay, B.C. in 1948.

Remarks: was named for York Township, Ont., but could not be given the actual name because of HMS *York*.

▼ *Runnymede in December, 1944.*

Runnymede at Montreal, not long before being commissioned in June 1944.

Viewed from a consort in 1944, **Runnymede** *wears the barber-pole stripes of EG C-5.*

ST. PIERRE

Builder: Davie Shipbuilding & Repairing Co. Ltd., Lauzon, Quebec.

Launched December 1, 1943.

Commissioned August 22, 1944 at Quebec City.

Wartime career: assigned in March 1945 to EG 9, Londonderry. Left Greenock on May 13 to escort a convoy to north Russia, but was detached to accompany 14 surrendered U-boats bound from Trondheim to Loch Eriboll. Returned to Canada in June and was paid off into reserve November 22, 1945.

Fate: sold in 1947 to the Peruvian Navy, to be renamed *Teniente Palacios* and, in 1953, *Palacios*. Broken up in 1966.

St. Pierre in the fall of 1944.

St. Pierre, 1944.

ST. STEPHEN

Builder: Yarrows Ltd., Esquimalt, B.C.

Launched February 6, 1944.

Commissioned July 28, 1944 at Esquimalt.

Wartime career: assigned in November to EG C-5, and spent the rest of the European war as a mid-ocean escort. Made nine trips across the Atlantic with convoys. Returned to Canada in June 1945 and was paid off into reserve November 22.

Postwar career: entered service as a weather ship in September 1947; stationed between Labrador and Greenland until August 1950. Sailed to Esquimalt, where she was paid off August 31 for loan to the Department of Transport. Transferred to the department in 1958 as a "spare" for sisters *St. Catharines* and *Stone Town,* also weather ships.

Fate: sold in 1968.

St. Stephen, August, 1944, shortly before leaving for the east coast.

▼ *Another view of the ship at about the same time.*

82

St. Stephen as a weather ship, 1947 - 50.

STE. THERESE

Builder: Davie Shipbuilding & Repairing Co. Ltd., Lauzon, Quebec.

Launched October 16, 1943.

Commissioned May 28, 1944 at Lévis.

Wartime career: joined EG 25 at Londonderry in November 1944, to serve in U.K. waters until February 1945, when she was reassigned to EG 28, Halifax. Carried out duties locally until paid off into reserve November 22. Recommissioned for training January 22, 1955, after being rebuilt as a Prestonian class escort. Paid off for the last time at Esquimalt, January 30, 1967.

Fate: broken up in Japan in 1967.

Ste. Thérèse in Prestonian configuration, on a visit to Japan, July 7, 1960.

Ste. Thérèse, August 28, 1944.

SEA CLIFF

Builder: Davie Shipbuilding & Repairing Co. Ltd., Lauzon, Quebec.

Launched July 8, 1944.

Commissioned September 26, 1944 at Quebec.

Wartime career: assigned in December 1944 to EG C-3, and spent the remainder of the European war as a mid-ocean escort. She escorted eight Atlantic convoys before returning to Canada in June 1945. Was paid off into reserve November 28.

Fate: sold in 1946 to the Chilean Navy and renamed *Covadonga,* she was broken up in 1968.

Remarks: was named for Leamington, Ont., whose actual name could not be used because of HMS *Leamington.*

*A dramatic photo of **Sea Cliff** from **Kokanee** in March 1945, when the two were escorting convoy SC.170.*

Sea Cliff on builder's trials in the St. Lawrence, September 1944.

STONE TOWN

Builder: Canadian Vickers Ltd., Montreal.

Launched March 28, 1944.

Commissioned July 21, 1944 at Montreal.

Wartime career: assigned in September 1944 as Senior Officer's ship to EG C-8. Spent the balance of the European war as a mid-ocean escort, making 12 Atlantic crossings. Returned to Canada in May 1945 and was paid off November 13.

Postwar career: sold to the Department of Transport and modified in 1950 for use as a weather ship. Served as such in the north Pacific, 1952 - 67.

Fate: sold in 1968.

Remarks: was named for Kingston, Ont., whose actual name could not be used because of HMS *Kingston*.

Stone Town in 1945, badly in need of paint.

▼ *Stone Town in June 1945.*

STRATHADAM

Builder: Yarrows Ltd., Esquimalt, B.C.

Launched March 20, 1944.

Commissioned September 29, 1944 at Victoria.

Wartime career: assigned in January 1945 to EG 25, Londonderry, and employed in U.K. waters until VE Day except for one trip to Gibraltar. On March 7, 1945, with *La Hulloise* and *Thetford Mines,* took part in sinking *U 1302* in St. George's Channel. Returned to Canada in May, and was paid off November 7.

Fate: sold to Uruguayan interests in 1947 but acquired by the Israeli Navy in 1950 and renamed *Misgav.* Broken up in 1959.

Remarks: was named for Newcastle, N.B., whose actual name could not be used because of HMS *Newcastle.*

◄ *Strathadam, early in life.*

Strathadam on the west coast, October 27, 1944.

SUSSEXVALE

Builder: Davie Shipbuilding & Repairing Co. Ltd., Lauzon, Quebec.

Launched July 12, 1944.

Commissioned November 29, 1944 at Quebec City.

Wartime career: joined EG 26 in Londonderry in March 1945 and spent the remainder of the war in U.K. waters. Returned to Canada after VE Day and was paid off November 16, 1945.

Postwar career: sold to Marine Industries Ltd. but reacquired for conversion to a Prestonian class escort and recommissioned as such March 18, 1955. Served in a training capacity until finally paid off November 30, 1966.

Fate: broken up in Japan in 1967.

Remarks: was named for Sussex, N.B., whose actual name could not be used because of HMS *Sussex*.

Sussexvale at Londonderry in the spring of 1945.

Sussexvale in the Channel, spring of 1945.

Sussexvale in June 1960, converted to a Prestonian class escort.

TORONTO

Builder: Davie Shipbuilding & Repairing Co. Ltd., Lauzon, Quebec.

Launched September 18, 1943.

Commissioned May 6, 1944 at Lévis.

Wartime career: operated on patrol and escort duty in Canadian waters until VE Day, when she began five months' service as a training ship at HMCS Cornwallis. Paid off November 27, 1945.

Postwar career: recommissioned March 26, 1953 after conversion to a Prestonian class escort. Paid off April 14, 1956 for loan to the Norwegian Navy, and renamed *Garm*. Permanently transferred in 1959 and reclassified in 1964 as a torpedo boat depot ship, at the same time being renamed *Valkyrien*. Discarded in 1977.

◄ *Toronto on September 14, 1954, modernized.*

Toronto, May 31, 1945, at HMCS Cornwallis.

VICTORIAVILLE

Builder: George T. Davie & Sons Ltd., Lauzon, Quebec.

Launched June 23, 1944.

Commissioned November 11, 1944 at Quebec City.

Wartime career: assigned in February 1945 to EG C-9, and spent the balance of the war as a mid-ocean escort. She made seven Atlantic crossings with convoys before returning to Canada in May 1945, and on May 12 escorted the surrendered *U 190* into Bay Bulls, Nfld. Was paid off November 17 and laid up at Shelburne.

Postwar career: was reacquired by the RCN from Marine Industries for conversion into a Prestonian class escort, recommissioning as such on September 25, 1959. In December 1966 she assumed the name and function of the retiring diving tender *Granby*. Paid off for the last time December 31, 1973, by then the last of the frigates still in service with the RCN.

Fate: sold for scrap in 1974.

Victoriaville, May 24, 1960, in Prestonian class guise.

▼ *Victoriaville in 1945*

EX-ROYAL NAVY RIVER CLASS

	wartime pendant		
ANNAN	K404	NENE	K270
ETTRICK	K254	RIBBLE	K525
MEON	K269	TEME	K458
MONNOW	K441		

Displacement: 2,216 tons (full load)

Dimensions: 301'6'' x 36'7'' x 12'9'' (mean)

Complement: 8 officers, 133 other ranks

Armament: 2 single 4-inch guns; 2 twin 20-mm guns, 2 single 20-mm guns; Hedgehog; 4 D.C. throwers, 2 traps, 150 - 200 depth charges.

ANNAN

Builder: Hall, Russell & Co., Abderdeen, Scotland.

Launched December 29, 1943.

Commissioned at Aberdeen, June 30, 1944.

Wartime career: transferred newly built from the RN and joined EG 6, Londonderry, in August 1944. Sank *U 1006* south of the Faeroes on October 16 while on A/S patrol. Transferred with her group to Halifax in April 1945 but returned to the U.K. at the end of May and was handed back to the RN on June 20.

Postwar career: sold to the Danish Navy in November 1945 and renamed *Niels Ebbesen*.

Fate: broken up at Odense, Denmark, in 1963.

Annan on September 25, 1944. The "gooseneck" whaler davits were the readiest means of distinguishing RN frigates from their RCN sisters. ▶

Annan, May 30, 1945.

92

Ettrick, likely in 1943 before her transfer to the RCN.

ETTRICK

Builder: John Crown & Sons, Sunderland, U.K.

Launched February 5, 1943.

Commissioned in the RCN January 29, 1944 at Halifax.

Wartime career: on transfer to the RCN, was assigned to EG C-3, and made two round trips as a mid-ocean escort before being reassigned to EG 27, Halifax. Was returned to the RN at Southampton on May 30, 1945.

Postwar career: converted to a Combined Operations Headquarters ship, then laid up in 1946.

Fate: broken up at Grays, Essex, in 1953.

◄ *Ettrick in December 1944.*

MEON

Builder: A. & J. Inglis Ltd., Glasgow, Scotland.

Launched August 4, 1943.

Commissioned in the RCN February 7, 1944 at Halifax.

Wartime career: assigned in May 1944 to EG 9, Londonderry, for patrol and escort in U.K. waters. Was present on D Day. Transferred to EG 27, Halifax, in October as Senior Officer's ship. Carried out various duties locally until returned to the RN at Southampton, April 23, 1945. Like *Ettrick*, was converted to a Combined Operations HQ ship.

Fate: broken up at Blyth in 1966.

Meon in May 1944.

Meon in July 1951, fitted as a Combined Operations H.Q. Ship.

Monnow in 1944, wearing unusual camouflage.

MONNOW

Builder: Charles Hill & Sons Ltd., Bristol, U.K.

Launched December 4, 1943.

Commissioned in the RCN at Bristol, March 8, 1944.

Wartime career: joined EG C-2 in May 1944 and made three round trips as a mid-ocean escort before being reassigned to EG 9, Londonderry. Made one round trip to Gibraltar and one to north Russia late in 1944. Was detached from another Murmansk convoy on May 13, 1945 to escort a large group of surrendered U-boats bound from Trondheim to Loch Eriboll. Was returned to the RN at Sheerness on June 11, 1945.

Postwar career: sold to the Danish Navy in October 1945 and renamed *Holger Dansk*.

Fate: broken up at Odense, Denmark, in 1959.

▼ *Monnow in a U.K. anchorage, 1944-45.*

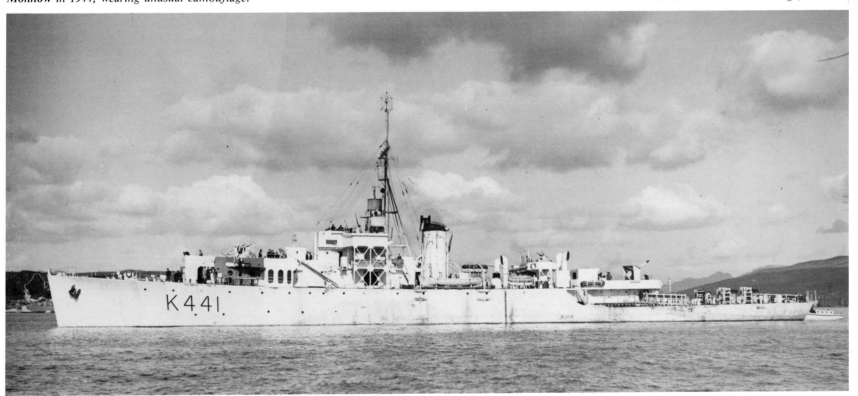

NENE

Builder: Smith's Dock Co., South Bank-on-Tees, U.K.

Launched December 9, 1942.

Wartime career: assigned, while still an RN ship, to Canadian escort group EG 5, based at St. John's. The group was renumbered EG 6 in November 1943, and *Nene* became its Senior Officer's ship in February 1944. On November 20, 1943, *Nene* shared with *Calgary* and *Snowberry* in the sinking of *U 536* north of the Azores. Was commissioned in the RCN at Halifax on April 6, 1944 and assigned in August, after working up, to EG C-5. Escorted three Atlantic convoys before reallocation in October to EG 9, Londonderry. Served in U.K. waters except for a trip to north Russia in December 1944. Recalled on May 16, 1945 from another Murmansk convoy to escort 14 surrendered U-boats en route from Trondheim to Loch Eriboll. Was handed back to the RN at Sheerness on June 12, 1945.

Fate: broken up at Briton Ferry, Wales, in 1955.

Nene in April 1943, while still an RN unit.

Nene from a consort, looking decidedly scruffy.

RIBBLE

Builder: Blyth Shipbuilding & Dry Dock Co. Ltd., Blyth, U.K.

Launched November 10, 1943.

Commissioned in the RCN, newly built, July 24, 1944, at Blyth.

Wartime career: assigned in August 1944 to EG 26, Londonderry, and spent her whole career in U.K. waters. Assisted in towing the damaged *Chebogue* to Swansea, Wales, October 7 - 9, 1944. Paid off at Sheerness June 11, 1945, for return to the RN.

Fate: broken up in 1957 at Blyth, U.K.

Ribble in 1944.

Ribble, 1944-45.

TEME

Builder: Smith's Dock Co., South Bank-on-Tees, U.K.

Launched November 11, 1943.

Commissioned February 28, 1944, at Middlesbrough.

Wartime career: assigned in May 1944 to EG 6, Londonderry, and spent her whole career with this group. Was present on D Day. Rammed and cut nearly in half by escort carrier *Tracker* in the Channel, June 10, 1944. Under repairs at Cardiff until the end of the year, and rejoined her group at Londonderry in February after working up. On March 29, 1945, was torpedoed by *U 246* off Falmouth, losing 60 feet of her stern. Declared a constructive total loss and paid off May 4.

Fate: broken up at Llanelly, Wales, in 1946.

Teme, 1945.

Teme, March 8, 1944.

98

	wartime pendant
LOCH ACHANALT	K424
LOCH ALVIE	K428
LOCH MORLICH	K517

Displacement: 2,260 tons (full load)

Dimensions: 307' x 38'6'' x 9'

Complement: 8 officers, 133 other ranks

Armament: 1 4-inch gun; 1 quad. 2-pdr. pompom; 2 twin 20-mm guns, 2 single 20-mm guns; 2 Squid mortars; 2 D.C. throwers, 1 trap.

LOCH ACHANALT

Builder: Henry Robb Ltd., Leith, Scotland.

Launched March 23, 1944.

Commissioned July 31, 1944 at Leith.

Wartime career: joined EG 6 at Londonderry in September. On patrol and escort duties in U.K. waters until VE Day. Accompanied the group to Halifax on its transfer there in April 1945, but returned in May to Sheerness and was returned to the RN on June 20.

Postwar career: sold to the Royal New Zealand Navy in 1948 and renamed *Pukaki*.

Fate: broken up at Hong Kong in 1966.

Loch Achanalt, a poor photo but one that provides good close-up detail.

Loch Achanalt in August 1944.

LOCH ALVIE

Builder: Barclay, Curle & Co. Ltd., Glasgow, Scotland.

Launched April 14, 1944.

Commissioned August 10, 1944 at Dalmuir.

Wartime career: joined EG 9, Londonderry, in September. Served in U.K. waters for the duration of the war except for a trip to Gibraltar in October and to Iceland in March 1944. Was detached, with *Monnow* and *Nene*, from a north Russian convoy on May 16, 1945, to escort 14 surrendered U-boats bound from Trondheim to Loch Eriboll. Was paid off at Sheerness on June 11 for return to the RN.

Postwar Career: recommissioned for service in the Far East, then laid up at Singapore, cannibalized for parts, and broken up in 1965.

Loch Alvie: a spirited study at sea.

Loch Alvie in Loch Eriboll, Scotland, May 19 or 20, 1945. The surrendered U 716 lies alongside.

LOCH MORLICH

Builder: Swan, Hunter & Wigham Richardson Ltd., Wallsend-on-Tyne, U.K.

Launched January 25, 1944.

Commissioned July 17, 1944 at Wallsend-on-Tyne.

Wartime career: joined EG 6 at Londonderry in September 1944 and remained with the group in U.K. waters until the end of the war. Accompanied the group to Halifax on April 25 on its transfer there, but returned at the end of May to Sheerness, and was there paid off June 20 for return to the RN.

Postwar career: was sold in 1949 to the Royal New Zealand Navy and renamed *Tutira*.

Fate: broken up at Hong Kong in 1966.

Loch Morlich in 1945. ►

Loch Morlich in 1944.

Loch Morlich *after the war. The most obvious differences from her River class consorts are the heavy lattice mast, topped by the "dish" antenna of a Type 277 radar; and the single Mark VIc 4-inch gun. The uneven deckline is a result of her prefabricated construction.*

ENVOI . . .

*Erstwhile foes resting from their labours: **U 889, U 190, Joliette, Thetford Mines** and **St. Catharines**, at Halifax on September 23, 1945.*

EXPLANATORY NOTES

References to convoys and escort groups are frequent in the book, and some explanation may be useful:

Eastbound convoys were designated "HX" or "SC". The former sailed initially from Halifax to the U.K., then (beginning in September 1942) from New York. The latter originated at first at Sydney, N.S., later at Halifax, and later still at New York. HX convoys were "fast", SC convoys "slow", meaning, in practical terms, 9 and 7-1/2 knots respectively. Westbound convoys, similarly, were designated "ON" and "ONS" — the former fast, the latter slow.

Escort groups C-1 to C-9 (C denoting "Canadian") were those which regularly escorted Atlantic convoys. Escort groups 6, 9, 15, 16 and 25 to 28 were "support groups" which functioned independently of the convoy cycle, but might be used to bolster the escort of beleaguered convoys when required. A particular function was that of patrolling the Western Approaches to the English Channel during and after D Day. Eleven RCN frigates of Escort Groups 6 and 9 were present at the Normandy landings of June 6, 1944.

Abbreviations used in the book are as follows:

A/S	Anti-Submarine
D.C.	Depth Charge
EG	Escort Group
HF/DF	High-Frequency Direction-Finding
W/T	Wireless Telegraphy (Radio)
Asdic	Acronym for the Anti-Submarine Detection Investigation Committee, which developed this equipment. It is now known as Sonar.

SELECTED BIBLIOGRAPHY

Easton, Alan. *50 North: An Alantic Battleground*. London: Eyre & Spottiswood, 1963.

Elliott, Peter. *Allied Escort Ships of World War II*. Annapolis: Naval Institute Press, 1977.

Hadley, Michael L. *U-Boats Against Canada*. Kingston and Montreal: McGill-Queen's University Press, 1985.

Lamb, James B. *On the Triangle Run*. Toronto: Macmillan, 1968.

Lenton, H.T. *British Escort Ships*. New York: Arco Publishing Co., 1974.

Macpherson, Ken and Burgess, John. *The Ships of Canada's Naval Forces, 1910-1985*. Toronto: Collins, 1985.

Milner, Marc. *North Atlantic Run*. Toronto: University of Toronto Press, 1985.

Schull, Joseph. *The Far Distant Ships*. Ottawa: D.N.D., 1952.

Tucker, Gilbert N. *The Naval Service of Canada, Vol. 2*. Ottawa: D.N.D., 1952.

PHOTO CREDITS

In selecting illustrations for this book I have, where possible, chosen photos seldom or, so far as I am aware, never before published. In a good many instances, considerations of quality have defeated this noble purpose, but I hope warship enthusiasts will find much that is new and unique.

In the list below, the negative numbers are those of official photographs held in the National Archives of Canada or the Canadian Forces Photographic Unit at Rockcliffe. In the latter case, the number will be prefaced "CFPU". The initials after the page numbers refer to the position of the illustrations on the pages in questions — upper, lower, etc.

I have acknowledged as many as I can of those lent to me by private individuals, but in a few cases have lost track of the benefactor's initials or, worse yet, his name. To these I apologize, and to all I extend my thanks.

72 L	B. Trumpour	96 U	Admiralty, U.K.
73 U	QS-0001-13	96 L	Parkway Productions
73 L	S.3393	97 U	Admiralty, U.K.
74 U	DNS.13025	97 L	CN.3806
74 L	MacRae	98 L	Admiralty, U.K.
75	S.3410	100 U	J.A.P. Clarke
76 U	CN.3527	100 L	C.S.J. Lancaster
76 L	R.A. Simon	101 U	W. Waycik
77 L	QS-0009-2	102 L	Admiralty, U.K.
78 U	F.W. McKee	103	Sport & General
78 L	CN.3283	104	Author's photo
79 L	K.434		
80 R	Norman James		
81 U	CN.6211		
81 L	CN.3625		
82 U	F.3232		
82 L	F.3229		
83	C.S.J. Lancaster		
84 U	Yasuo Abe		
84 L	HS.0753-4		
85 U	Don Warren		
85 L	0.660-1		
86 U	R.A. Simon		
86 L	Z.1578		
87 U	Bruce		
87 L	F.4026		
88 LL	C.S.J. Lancaster		
88 LR	CFPU E.56578		
89 U	MAG.5956		
89 L	DB.0720		
90 U	CFPU DNS.25652		
90 L	CN.3652		
92 U	Admiralty, U.K.		
92 L	HS.0343-119		
93 U	S.2881		
93 L	Admiralty, U.K.		
94 U	S.423		
94 L	Wright & Logan		
95 L	Imperial War Museum		